D1682817

Copyright © 1991 by Running Press.

Printed and bound in the United States. All rights reserved under the Pan-American and International Copyright Conventions.
This book may not be reproduced in whole or in part in any form or by any means, electronic or mechanical, including photocopying, recording, or by any information storage and retrieval system now known or hereafter invented, without written permission from the publisher.
Canadian representatives: General Publishing Co., Ltd., 30 Lesmill Road, Don Mills, Ontario M3B 2T6.
International representatives: Worldwide Media Services, Inc., 115 East Twenty-third Street, New York, New York 10010.
ISBN 1-56138-012-1
Cover design by Toby Schmidt
Interior design by Stephanie Longo
Research by Amy Gahran
Cover illustration by Stacey Lewis
Background photos courtesy of NASA and Jet Propulsion Laboratory
Typography by Commcor Communications Corporation, Philadelphia, Pennsylvania

This book may be ordered by mail from the publisher. Please add $2.50 for postage and handling.
But try your bookstore first!
Running Press,
125 South Twenty-second Street, Philadelphia, Pennsylvania 19103.

The Stargazer's Diary

. . . fire is the silent language of
the star.

CONRAD AIKEN (1889–1973)
American poet and critic

The surface of the earth is the shore of the cosmic ocean.

CARL SAGAN, b. 1934
American astronomer, physicist, and writer

On a clear, moonless night in midwinter or midsummer, a plume of starlight rises motionless behind the scattering of constellations.... The Milky Way is our island universe....

CHARLES A. WHITNEY, b. 1929
American astronomer and writer

This is a new ocean, and I believe [we] must sail upon it.

**JOHN FITZGERALD KENNEDY
(1917–1963)**
35th President of the United States

Like the fifteenth-century navigators, astronomers today are embarked on voyages of exploration, charting unknown regions. The aim of this adventure is to bring back not gold or spices or silks but something more valuable: a map of the universe that will tell of its origins, its texture, and its fate.

ROBERT P. KIRSHNER, b. 1949
American astrophysicist and educator

Come...and I shall tell the beginnings of the sun, and the sources from which have sprung all the things we now behold....

EMPEDOCLES (493–433 B.C.)
Greek philosopher and statesman

Science is what you know, philosophy is what you don't know.

BERTRAND RUSSELL (1872–1970)
British philosopher and teacher

At first astronomy, like other sciences, was studied mainly for utilitarian reasons. It provided a measure of time and enabled mankind to keep a tally of the flight of the seasons; it taught him to find his way across the trackless desert, and later, the trackless ocean.

SIR JAMES JEANS, F.R.S.
(1877–1946)
British astronomer and writer

A wise man
Watching the stars pass across
 the sky,
Remarked:
In the upper air the fireflies
 move more slowly.

> **AMY LOWELL (1874–1925)**
> American poet and critic

There is a geometry in the humming of the strings. There is music in the spacings of the spheres.

PYTHAGORAS (582–507 B.C.)
Greek philosopher and mathematician

The morning stars sang together.

THE BOOK OF JOB

Plato believed that anything and everything conceivable exists somewhere in the universe....

MICHAEL GUILLEN, b. 1950
American mathematician

Nothing is fixed, that mortals
 see or know
Unless perhaps some stars
 be so....

JONATHAN SWIFT (1667–1745)
English churchman and writer

Hast thou a charm to stay the
  morning star
In his steep course?

**SAMUEL TAYLOR COLERIDGE
(1772–1834)**
English poet, writer, and critic

Bright Star! Would I were as steadfast as thou art!

JOHN KEATS (1795–1821)
English poet

Farewell, Morning Star, herald of dawn, and quickly come as the Evening Star, bringing again in secret her whom thou takest away.

MELEAGER (1st century B.C.)
Greek epigrammist

To see the world in a grain
   of sand,
And a heaven in a wild flower;
Hold infinity in the palm of
   your hand,
And eternity in an hour.

WILLIAM BLAKE (1757–1827)
   English artist, poet, and mystic

There is one glory of the sun,
and another glory of the moon,
and another glory of the stars:
for one star differeth from
another star in glory.

I CORINTHIANS

Man is his own star, and the
   soul that can
Render an honest and a perfect
   man
Commands all light, all influ-
   ence, all fate.
Nothing to him falls early, or
   too late.
Our acts our angels are, or good
   or ill,
Our fatal shadows that walk by
   us still.

JOHN FLETCHER (1597–1625)
English dramatist

"If thou," he answered, "follow but thy star,
Thou canst not miss at last a glorious haven."

DANTE ALIGHIERI (1265–1321)
Italian poet

We had the sky up there, all speckled with stars, and we used to lay on our backs and look up at them, and discuss about whether they were made, or only just happened.

MARK TWAIN (1835–1910)
American writer

Men love to wonder, and that is the seed of science.

**RALPH WALDO EMERSON
(1803–1882)**
American philosopher, essayist,
and poet

Touch a scientist and you touch a child.

RAY BRADBURY, b. 1920
American writer

Let there be lights in the firmament of the heavens to divide the day from the night.

GENESIS

Silently, one by one, in the infinite meadows of Heaven Blossomed the lovely stars, the forget-me-nots of the angels....

HENRY WADSWORTH LONGFELLOW (1807–1882)
American poet

Heaven and Earth are as old as I, and the ten thousand things are one.

CHUANG TZU (4th century B.C.)
Chinese philosopher and poet

What art was to the ancient world, science is to the modern.

BENJAMIN DISRAELI
(1804–1881)
English statesman and writer

Where the telescope ends, the microscope begins. Which of the two has the grander view?

VICTOR HUGO (1802–1885)
French novelist

I ask you to look both ways. For the road to a knowledge of the stars leads through the atom; and important knowledge of the atom has been reached through the stars.

SIR ARTHUR STANLEY EDDINGTON (1882–1944)
English astronomer

Stars are like animals in the wild. We may see the young but never the actual birth, which is a veiled and secret event.

HEINZ R. PAGELS (1939–1988)
American physicist and writer

Stars scribble in our eyes the
   frosty sagas,
The gleaming cantos of unvan-
   quished space.

HART CRANE (1899–1932)
American poet

I will hide myself among you,
O ye stars which are imperishable.

A N I (c. 4,000 B.C.)
Author of *The Book of the Dead*

One could not pluck a flower without troubling a star.

LOREN EISELEY (1907–1977)
American anthropologist

There was a star danced, and under that I was born.

**WILLIAM SHAKESPEARE
(1564–1616)**
English poet and playwright

Oh, write of me, not "Died in
bitter pains,"
But "Emigrated to another
star!"

**HELEN HUNT JACKSON
(1831–1885)**
American writer

We have loved the stars too
fondly to be fearful of the night.

EPITAPH OF AN AMATEUR ASTRONOMER

It is possible that our race may be an accident, in a meaningless universe, living its brief life uncared for, on this dark, cooling star: but even so—and all the more—what marvelous creatures we are!

CLARENCE DAY (1874–1935)
American writer

And they know neither sect nor idolatry, with the exception that all believe that the source of all power and goodness is in the sky. . . .

**CHRISTOPHER COLUMBUS
(1451–1506)**
Italian explorer

Put three grains of sand inside a vast cathedral, and the cathedral will be more closely packed with sand than space is with stars.

SIR JAMES JEANS, F.R.S.
(1877–1946)
British astronomer and writer

It is indeed an exacting requirement to have to ascribe physical reality to space in general, and especially to empty space.

ALBERT EINSTEIN (1879–1955)
German-American physicist

A single lifetime, even though entirely devoted to the sky, would not be enough for the investigation of so vast a subject.

SENECA (c. 4 B.C.–39 A.D.)
Roman philosopher and statesman

If I have been able to see farther than others, it was because I stood on the shoulders of giants.

SIR ISAAC NEWTON (1642–1727)
English mathematician, scientist, and philosopher

No sight that the human eyes can look upon is more provocative of awe than is the night sky scattered thick with stars.

LLEWELYN POWYS (1884–1939)
English essayist and writer

I could have gone on flying
through space forever.

YURI GAGARIN (1934–1968)
Soviet cosmonaut, first person
to fly in space

Here he was adrift in this great river of suns, halfway between the banked fires of the galactic core and the lonely, scattered sentinel stars of the rim. And *here* he wished to be, on the far side of this chasm in the sky, this serpentine band of darkness, empty of all stars.

ARTHUR C. CLARKE, b. 1917
American writer

I have no watch nor sentinel but what the stars keep for me.

MICHEL EYQUEM DE MONTAIGNE (1533–1592)
French essayist

Our sun is one of 100 billion stars in our galaxy. Our galaxy is one of billions of galaxies populating the universe. It would be the height of presumption to assume that we are the only living things in this enormous immensity.

WERNHER VON BRAUN
(1912–1977)
German-American rocket engineer

Stars are to be looked at with the eye, not reached at with the hand.

ROBERT GREENE (1558–1592)
English poet and playwright

Of late, contemplating the heavens has become an even more humbling experience than ever.

MARCIA BARTUSIAK, b. 1952
American writer

We owe our corporeal existence
to events that took place billions
of years ago, in stars that lived
and died long before the solar
system came into being.

ROBERT JASTROW, b. 1925
American astronomer

Both the man of science and the man of action live always at the edge of mystery, surrounded by it.

J. ROBERT OPPENHEIMER
(1904–1967)
American physicist

Everything that physicists have learned about the natural world invites us to accept uncertainty.

MICHAEL GUILLEN, b. 1950
American mathematician

There is no easy road from the earth to the stars.

SENECA (c. 4 B.C.–39 A.D.)
Roman philosopher and statesman

What is it that makes a man willing to sit up on top of an enormous Roman candle... and wait for someone to light the fuse?

TOM WOLFE, b. 1931
American writer

I knew I was alone in a way that no earthling has ever been before.

MICHAEL COLLINS, b. 1930
United States astronaut, reflecting on his solo flight in lunar orbit

> Men who have worked together to reach the stars are not likely to descend together to the depths of war and desolation.
>
> **LYNDON B. JOHNSON**
> (1908–1973)
> 36th President of the United States

The message from the moon which we have flashed to the far corners of this planet is that no problem need any longer be considered insoluble.

NORMAN COUSINS, b. 1912
American writer and editor

The realization that our small planet is only one of many worlds gives mankind the perspective it needs to realize sooner that our own world belongs to all of its creatures, that the moon landing marks the end of our childhood as a race and the beginning of a newer and better civilization.

ARTHUR C. CLARKE, b. 1917
American writer

Problems . . . look mighty small from 150 miles up.

ROGER CHAFFEE (1935–1967)
United States astronaut

If you wish to make an apple pie from scratch, you must first invent the universe.

CARL SAGAN, b. 1934
American astronomer, physicist, and writer

A day will come, one day in the unending succession of days, when beings who are now latent in our thoughts and hidden in our loins shall stand upon this earth as one stands upon a footstool, and shall laugh and reach out their hands amidst the stars.

H. G. WELLS (1866–1946)
English novelist, sociologist, and historian